THIS JOURNAL
BELONGS TO

Allison Nicole Rohr

3/22/16

A
LITTLE
GOD
TIME

DEVOTIONAL JOURNAL

BELLE
CITY
GIFTS

BroadStreet Publishing Group LLC
Racine, Wisconsin, USA
Broadstreetpublishing.com

A LITTLE GOD TIME

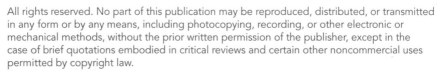

© 2016 by BroadStreet Publishing

ISBN 978-1-4245-5222-1

Design by Chris Garborg | www.garborgdesign.com
Edited and compiled by Michelle Winger | www.literallyprecise.com
Cover and interior image © Bigstock/lozas

Printed in China.

16   17   18   19   20   21   22   7   6   5   4   3   2   1

*The L*ORD *is good to those*
whose hope is in him,
to the one who seeks him;
it is good to wait quietly
*for the salvation of the L*ORD.

Lamentations 3:25-26 NIV

INTRODUCTION

When everything else in life demands your attention, rest in the Lord to find the hope, joy, and peace you need each day.

This one-year devotional provides you with godly wisdom and insight to strengthen your faith and encourage your spirit.

The Father is captivated by you! He delights in every moment you choose to spend with him. Let your heart be filled with his presence and find the peace that is abundant there.

Be refreshed and inspired as you make
A Little God Time part of your day.

THE FATHER'S LOVE

Regardless of how beautifully or how imperfectly your earthly father showed his love, your heavenly Father's love is utterly boundless. Rest in that thought a moment. There is nothing you can do to change how he feels about you. *Nothing.*

We spend so much time trying to make ourselves more lovable, from beauty regimens to gourmet baking, to being there for pretty much everyone. It's easy to forget we are already perfectly loved. Our Father loves us more than we can imagine. And he would do anything for us. *Anything.*

> *"If a man has a hundred sheep but one of the sheep gets lost, he will leave the other ninety-nine on the hill and go to look for the lost sheep. I tell you the truth, if he finds it he is happier about that one sheep than about the ninety-nine that were never lost."*
>
> Matthew 18:12-13 NCV

Who do you love most fiercely, most protectively, most desperately here on earth? What would you do for them? Know that it's a mere fraction, nearly immeasurable, of what God would do for you. Spend some time thanking him for his great love.

*Read Matthew ✓
Chs. 17-19

Tuesday March 22, 2016

Last night was incredible! I made 2 new friends at the women's Bible Study, had my meal paid for, received healing / healing oil, prayer, encouragement, and this journal. Thank you Lord!!!! ♡ Thank you Father for supplying above and beyond my needs. I praise you Jesus. This morning I am thankful for friends being willing to lend a hand, when a hand is needed the most! My car is currently in the shop and I needed a ride to work this morning. Thank you Lord for Arianna and her selflessness being so kind and willing to help me out today. Lord I ask that you bless and pour out on Avi and bring an abundant love and peace over her. Readjust her eyes and thoughts back on you Jesus. Allow her circumstances to grow silent and fade because you are in control.

GROWTH

Do you remember when you realized you had stopped growing? Your height was going to be your height, your shoe size your shoe size. This second fact was pretty thrilling for many of us; no more hearing Mom say, "That's too much to spend on shoes you'll outgrow in a few months." And so the collection began.

Not too long after our bones finish growing, we realize the real growth is just getting started. As we become young women, friendships either deepen or fade away as we begin to figure out who we are. No matter what our ages today, most of us are still working on that one. When we are growing in Christ, it's a process that never really ends.

> *I do not mean that I am already as God wants me to be.*
> *I have not yet reached that goal, but I continue trying to*
> *reach it and to make it mine. Christ wants me to do that,*
> *which is the reason he made me his.*
>
> Philippians 3:12 NCV

How does knowing that God wants to help you become your best inspire you to attempt it?

Wednesday March 23, 2016
When I think about God wanting
actually wanting to help me become my
best I feel so loved and cherished!
I am reassured that God is
looking at my heart and best interest
in mind. He is always having time
for me, even when I am unfaithful.
This all inspires me to attempt it
(becoming my best), because that's what
Jesus would do. I want to be
fully surrendered to God at all
times, making a constant effort to
be balanced in all areas, taking every
chance I can get to deepen my intimate
relationship with God, making myself disciplined
by keeping God at #1 priority, & having
a heart of gratitude, serving and loving
wholeheartedly, and taking every day to
know God in a new, and fun way!
Then after this, I ask God to reveal to me!

who He wants me to mentor, reach out, and pour into. Thank you Lord for always being there for me.

FOLLOW THE ARROW

Decisions, decisions. It seems a week never goes by without our needing to make at least one important choice. Whether job related, relationship motivated, or something as seemingly innocent as how to spend a free Friday, wouldn't it be nice to have an arrow pointing us in the right direction—especially if we are in danger of making a wrong turn?

According to the Word, we have exactly that. When we truly desire to walk the path God sets us on, and when we earnestly seek his voice, he promises to lead us in the right direction. His ever-present Spirit is right there, ready to put us back on the path each time we wander off.

> Your ears shall hear a word behind you, saying,
> "This is the way, walk in it,"
> Whenever you turn to the right hand
> or whenever you turn to the left."
>
> Isaiah 30:21 NKJV

Consider the decisions before you right now. To whom are you turning for guidance? Lay your options before God, and then listen for his voice.

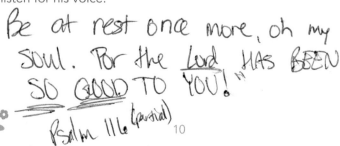

"Be at rest once more, oh my soul. For the Lord, HAS BEEN SO GOOD TO YOU!"
Psalm 116 (partial)

10

YOU CAN HAVE IT ALL LORD!

Sunday, March 27, 2016

Happy Easter!! Jesus is ALIVE!!!
Thank you Lord for dying on the
cross for my sins. Thank you
for sacrificing yourself for me. This
is a kind, humble, and chivalrous
act to carry out. Lord thank you
for telling me, "Beloved you are
ALWAYS worth it! Getting to see all
of my family this weekend was a
sweet and faithful opportunity. Thank you
Jesus. As I sit here in my bed
at my parent's house I am just
relaxed. Hearing the rain tap ever so gently
on my roof brings a lot of peace to
my mind and heart. Lord I thank
you for always making me feel welcomed
back when I journal or & soak in your
Presence. I surrender to you again
Lord and loving Father. I trust you lord and
Lord I welcome you into every area of my life.

Lord you already intimate with

hidden or withheld from you!!! I want to grow so much more o

Every area. nothing and I see it all and
you.

YOU ARE PERFECT

Stop, go back, and read that again. You are perfect. Looking in the mirror, or thinking back over your day, it is easy to forget or disbelieve those words. Don't let that happen. A wrinkle here, a bulge there, an unkind word, or a jealous thought cannot change the way the Father sees you. And it's how he wants you to see yourself.

The dictionary uses 258 words to explain what it means to be perfect, but we only need to know this: We are *complete*. When he chose to die on the cross for our sins, Jesus took away every flaw from those of us who love him. He finished what we never could; he made us perfect.

> By a single offering he has perfected for all time those who are being sanctified.
>
> Hebrews 10:14 ESV

Stand before a mirror and ask God to show you what he sees when he looks at you. See past the flaws, past any hurt or anger in your eyes, past any perceived imperfection. See yourself complete, just as you were meant to be. See yourself perfect. How does this change the way you feel about yourself?

*Have faith to know the blueprints!

In the process remind yourself— who started it and who's going to finish & walk through it with you.

Tuesday, March 29, 2016
As I stand before a mirror
I ask God, "Show me what You
see when You look at me?" He said
    I'm Making Progress Pt.2 9/27/16
Living a Life Holy Spirit Led
    By Carl Lentz
Jesus → Great Physician
  Holy Spirit → Great Physical Therapist
   Teaches us how to walk again.
1) How are you handling your own sin?
• Matth. 5
2) You can expect the unbelievable and
   unearned restoration.
• Eph. 3:25 → Not for our glory but for His!
Problems → potential opportunities for supernatural
moves of God. A moment to see God like
you never have.   Progress leads to platform.
* You can't choose the season you're in
   but you _can_ choose the spirit with
   which you walk through it.

YOU ARE CHERISHED

It's good to be loved, isn't it? What feeling really compares to knowing someone has run through the rain, cancelled an international flight, driven all night—for you? Even if we've never experienced it, we've imagined it in our hearts. Or else we've had the realization that we, too, would move heaven and earth for the one we love the most. Whether husband, child, parent, sibling, or dear friend, to love and be loved deeply just may be the best feeling there is.

How much love you have given or received is a mere sampling of the way Jesus feels about you. You are cherished, loved beyond reason or measure. The one who really *can* move heaven and earth would do so in a heartbeat—for you.

> *I am convinced that neither death nor life, neither angels nor demons, neither the present nor the future, nor any powers, neither height nor depth, nor anything else in all creation, will be able to separate us from the love of God that is in Christ Jesus our Lord.*
>
> Romans 8:38-39 NIV

Let the incredible words above wash over you as you realize there is nothing—absolutely nothing—Jesus wouldn't do for you. Can you feel his love toward you today?

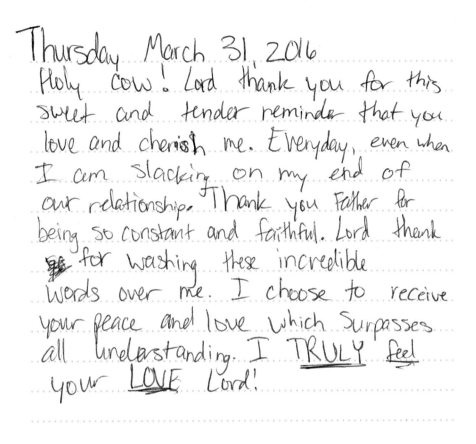

Thursday March 31, 2016

Holy cow! Lord thank you for this sweet and tender reminder that you love and cherish me. Everyday, even when I am slacking on my end of our relationship. Thank you Father for being so constant and faithful. Lord thank ~~you~~ for washing these incredible words over me. I choose to receive your peace and love which surpasses all understanding. I TRULY feel your LOVE Lord!

TROUBLED HEART

I can't get a moment's peace. Sound familiar? We all go through seasons where it seems every corner hides a new challenge to our serenity, assuming we've actually achieved any semblance of serenity in the first place. Why is it so hard to find peace in this world? Because we're looking *in this world*.

After his resurrection, before Jesus ascended into heaven, he left his disciples with something they'd never had before: peace. More specifically, he gave them *his* peace, a gift not of this world. Whatever the world can offer us can also be taken from us. Any security, happiness, or temporary reprieve from suffering is just that: temporary. Only the things of heaven are permanent and cannot be taken away.

> *"Peace I leave with you; my peace I give you. I do not give to you as the world gives. Do not let your hearts be troubled and do not be afraid."*
>
> John 14:27 NIV

Do not *let* your heart be troubled, Jesus tells us. This means we have a choice. Share the things with him that threaten your peace, and then remember they have no hold on you. You are his, and his peace is yours. How can you choose peace in your situation today?

September 24, 2016

In my situation today, I am going to trust the Lord with the plans and promises for my life. I am going to choose peace by leaving these burdens or thoughts at Jesus' feet where they belong and not in my head. I also can choose peace by inviting the Holy Spirit to have His way in my life today.

The Lord told me, "Though the seasons change,

~ ♡ MY LOVE REMAINS! ♡ ~

He also asked, "How are you doing my beloved?"

God also said, "Just like a weather man or woman predicts the weather I sometimes try to predict my future and try to figure it all out. Just trust Me and don't worry. I've got you love."

Patience + Persistence + Perseverance = PAYOFF + PRIZE!

HEARING GOD

The best way to know if something is true, or right, is to hear it for yourself—straight from the source. You believe you nailed the interview, but you don't believe you got the job until you get the phone call. The same is true for bad news, at least ideally. You get wind of a rumor about a friend's indiscretion, but you wait for her side of the story before believing a word.

So what about God? How can we hear from him? How do we discern his will for our lives? We may not have a hotline, but we do have his book. God speaks to us through his Word, so if you are waiting for confirmation, direction, validation, or conviction, pick it up. Read, and listen.

> *So faith comes from hearing,*
> *and hearing through the word of Christ.*
>
> Romans 10:17 ESV

How often do you feel God speaking to you through his Word? Are your conversations as frequent and meaningful as you'd like? Share you heart with him right now, and listen for his reply.

September 25, 2016

Whenever I am in God's Word I can feel the words come to life right off the page. Lord help me to talk to you more and welcome you into ~~this~~ all areas of my life. I invite you Holy Spirit to dwell in me and control my thoughts, words, and actions. Lord I want our convos to be 24/7 constant and clear. Lord I lay down all my rights and say I give you this day. Have your way, in me, I trust you and choose you.

Alli,

It's going to be Me and you forever and always. Keep trusting Me and My timing daughter. I love you and only want what's best for you dear one.

Always,

There's no space between Jesus
you and Me.

19

NOTHING TO FEAR

A loud crash in the night. Unexpected footsteps falling uncomfortably close in a dark parking lot. A ringing phone at 3:00 AM. No matter how brave we think we are, certain situations quicken the pulse. We've heard, over and over, that we have nothing to fear if we walk with God, but let's be honest: certain situations are scary! So what does it mean to have nothing to fear?

Let's consider David's words from Psalm 56. When we are afraid, and we will be, we can give our situation to God and let him take the fear away. Notice it doesn't say he changes the situation, but that he changes our response to it. We have nothing to fear not because scary things don't exist, but because God erases our worry and replaces it with trust.

> In the day that I'm afraid, I lay all my fears before you
> and trust in you with all my heart.
> What harm could a man bring to me?
> With God on my side I will not be afraid of what comes.
>
> Psalm 56:3-4 TPT

What are you afraid of? Have you truly tried letting go of that fear? If not, why? Talk to God about it now.

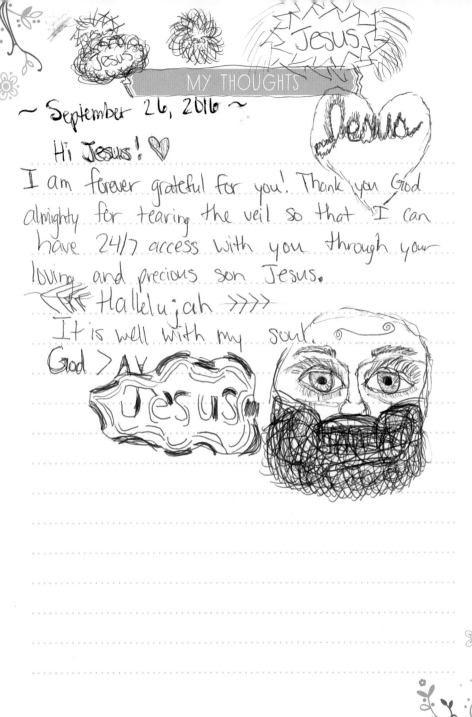

MY THOUGHTS

JESUS

Jesus

~ September 26, 2016 ~

Hi Jesus! ♥

I am forever grateful for you! Thank you God almighty for tearing the veil so that I can have 24/7 access with you through your loving and precious son Jesus.
Hallelujah >>>>
It is well with my soul.
God > AV

Jesus

THE PATIENCE PIT

We're not that good at waiting for anything these days. Yet, the reality is that waiting is a necessary part of life. We wait for people, we wait for events, and we wait for desires to be fulfilled. But do we recognize that waiting might also apply to our emotional lives? Do we hold on to hope that we can be rescued from a troubled heart?

King David described himself as being in a pit of miry clay, likely another of his despairing moments, perhaps even on reflection of his sins. He needed to be rescued, not necessarily from his enemies, but from his state of mind. David says he *waited patiently*, understanding that he might not be instantly rescued. And he trusted that God alone would save him.

> I waited and waited and waited some more;
> patiently, knowing God would come through for me.
> Then, at last, he bent down and listened to my cry.
>
> Psalm 40:11 TPT

Do you feel as though your emotions are on slippery ground or that your thoughts are stuck in the miry clay? Are you willing to wait patiently for the great rescuer to lift you up and place your feet on solid ground? Take a moment today to ask God for his help, recognize the necessity of waiting, and trust him for the rescue.

• I desire to do your will, O my God; your law is within my heart.
Psalm 40:8 •

September 27, 2016

What does patience mean to me?
Ans. Patience is the self-discipline of being willing to positively and persistently wait for with a humble expectation for something over a period of time.

What does process mean?
Ans. Process is the time with which the patience endures, shapening occurs, and ~~and go~~ lessons are learned and growth is evident. Hope is built and lifted, faith is stretched, and intimacy is fueled and strengthened with Jesus. Vulnerability is transparent and trust is rooted ~~through~~ in God. Motivation is engaged by grit that says, "Nothing and no one, not even myself, can shake me or break me. The realization that you go from glory to glory and grace to grace. You discover the vitality for fruitful friendships and the pruning of limp or dead limbs. STAY CONNECTED TO THE VINE! Always remember, I'M MAKING PROGRESS! 23

CREATURES OF HABIT

Wake up. Make bed. Get dressed. Coffee. Not always in that order, but you can guarantee that many do those things every single morning. They might also bite their nails, anger easily, and stay up too late. Patterns are hard to break. We are, after all, creatures of habit, and unfortunately not all of those habits are good.

What do you do when you are confronted with a habit that is not positive? Do you recognize when you rely on something just because it makes you feel accepted, comforted, or in control? Sometimes we aren't even conscious of our habits until we try to give them up.

Scripture says that establishing the right pattern begins with the renewing of our minds. This means that we must first acknowledge the need for change, and then submit our way of thinking to resemble that of Christ.

Do not conform to the pattern of this world, but be transformed by the renewing of your mind. Then you will be able to test and approve what God's will is—his good, pleasing and perfect will.

Romans 12:2 NIV

What habits do you find yourself constantly trying to break? Can you trust God today to show you his good, pleasing, and perfect will as you submit your worldly patterns to him?

September 28, 2016

Habits I have:

- Not checking my finances daily
- Right now, not studying as often for my pharmacy tech. license
- Staying up late
- Eating sugar + not healthy
- Getting behind on laundry + putting clothes away
- Not using my gift of tongues
- Barely working out
- Limited communication w/ God throughout the day
- Getting offended by my dad

Lord I lay each of these habits at your feet today. I trust you God and I am willing to let you show me your good, pleasing, and perfect will. Holy Spirit come! I welcome you and invite you as the Advocate to convict, correct, and counsel me in every area of my life.

MEDITATE ON GOODNESS

Do you ever catch yourself dwelling on the negative aspects of life? We can be nonchalant when someone tells us good news, but talk for hours about conflict, worries, and disappointment. It is good to communicate things that aren't going so well in our lives, but we can also fall into the trap of setting our minds on the wrong things.

Paul saw the need to address this within the church of Philippi. It seems there were people in the church that thought too highly of themselves and allowed discord to reside in their midst. Think of what dwelling on the negative actually does: it creates feelings of hopelessness, discouragement, and a lack of trust in our God who is good, true, and just.

> *Whatever is true, whatever is honorable, whatever is right, whatever is pure, whatever is lovely, whatever is of good repute, if there is any excellence and if anything worthy of praise, dwell on these things.*
>
> Philippians 4:8 NASB

Can you find anything in your life and the lives of others that have virtue or are worthy of praise? Choose to dwell on the true, noble, just, pure, and lovely things, and experience the refreshing nature of a positive outlook.

September 30, 2016

Happy 1 week devotionaliversary! I have consistently and ambitiously ~~been~~ spent time with ~~E~~ the Lord and in His Word for 1 whole week! And I ~~LOVE IT! 🖤 🖤 🖤🖤 ~~ ~ ~

One man I know right off the bat that is full of virtue, honor, thanksgiving, blessing, respect, awe, glory, and praise, a WELL SPRING OF LIFE is JESUS! I could talk about Him for hours on end and I am immediately lifted and full of hope, love, and fire again! Overflowing in fact! Jesus touching my heart at the age of 5 and continuing to be there through ↑'s and ↓'s He is CONSTANT and never moves! Jesus has shown me His love through fruitful friendships, sisters and brothers of Christ, throughout my lifetime.

FULLY TRUSTING

*T*rust can be a hard word to put into action mostly because our experience with others tells us that we can be sorely disappointed. People let us down in many ways. We can even be disappointed in ourselves.

Remember the trust game that involved standing with eyes closed and falling back into the hands of a few peers in hopes that they would catch you? There was risk involved in that game, and it didn't always turn out well. Nothing can truly be guaranteed in this life, can it? Well, it depends on where you place your trust.

> *Trust in the Lord with all your heart,*
> *And lean not on your own understanding;*
> *In all your ways acknowledge Him,*
> *And He shall direct your paths.*

> Proverbs 3:5-6 NKJV

God watches over us, cares for us, and is involved in our lives. When we acknowledge that every good thing comes from him, our faith is strengthened and we are able to trust him more. Make a point of noticing how God directs your paths today, and thank him for being trustworthy.

October 1, 2016

~ Hello October! ~

Lord I thank you for creating me. Thank you for another day! Help me oh God to make a point of acknowledging how you direct my paths today, and that every good thing comes from you. Lord I trust you as Father, Friend, and Lord with my life and everything you want to do in me and through me. I say, "Yes Lord!" With a cheerful heart, mind, and attitude. I love you Lord!

LOVE WITHOUT FEAR

God is an awesome God. He is all-powerful and he is holy. When we compare ourselves to such greatness, we can be overwhelmed with our insignificance. God is the author of life and death, and he determines our eternity!

But we know that God is love, and because of his love, he created a way for us to approach him boldly. He made us righteous and holy through the redemption of Christ. We are no longer in fear of punishment from a powerful God. Human love can involve fear because it is not perfect. It can disappoint, it can be taken away, and it can create a power imbalance that highlights our insecurities.

> *There is no fear in love. But perfect love drives out fear, because fear has to do with punishment. The one who fears is not made perfect in love.*
>
> 1 John 4:18 NIV

Do you compare God's love for you with the earthly love you have experienced? Acknowledge your struggle to accept God's perfect love. Allow yourself to love, and to be loved, without fear.

· Saturday, July 29, 2017 ·

Something about Saturday mornings, Jesus. ♡ Being alive, soaking in Your Presence, breaking bread and fellowshipping with you, listening for your sweet soft, peacefilled voice. Just spending time, hours upon hours with you satisfies my every fiber of being. ♥ Taste and see that You are Good! Your love endures forever! Thank you Lord. I love you Jesus. You are always kind, patient, loving, tender, holy, gracefilled, the best friend, full of mercy (covenant-keeping love), dreamy, full of forgiveness, hold no record of wrongs, humble, joyfilled, Steadfast, friend, faithful, provider, teacher, sacrificial, Selfless, intimate, Strong, amazing, hopefilled, thankful Sovereign, prince of peace, majestic, and so much more! Never ending! "I will never desert you, nor will I ever forsake you" - Hebrews 13:5

Things to pray about: - Husband
- Deeper intimacy with Jesus   - Family
- Being aware + inviting Holy Spirit - Monte, Beth's grandparents + Beth
- Faith   - A new job
                                - Move to NY this fall to save for BSSM
                                - Youth, awakened harts
                                    work place coworkers

PERFECT IN WEAKNESS

Have you ever taken a personality test to identify your strengths and weaknesses? You probably know if you are an introvert or extravert, whether you are creative or administrative, good at speaking, or great at listening. You probably also know all too well what your weaknesses are. You might be over-analytical, self-doubting, unorganized, or lacking empathy. There are areas in our life that we certainly don't feel proud of!Paul, on the other hand, says he would rather boast about his weaknesses! Paul knew that his weaknesses made him rely on the power of the Holy Spirit.

> "My grace is sufficient for you, for power is perfected in weakness." Most gladly, therefore, I will rather boast about my weaknesses, so that the power of Christ may dwell in me.
>
> 2 Corinthians 12:9 NASB

Make Himself at home; forever like and remain.

You may be facing something that you are worried about because it is outside of your comfort zone. It is not really the weakness in which you boast, but rather the power of Christ that is revealed through your weakness. Will you consider that God can shine through you as you acknowledge your complete reliance on his Holy Spirit?

October 4, 2016

"My grace is SUFFICIENT for you, for power is perfected in weakness." Most GLADLY, therefore, I will rather boast about my weaknesses, so that the power of CHRIST MAY DWELL IN ME.
2 Cor. 12:9

Lord,
      You are so good! Thank you for showing me that you can shine through me as I acknowledge my complete reliance on your Holy Spirit. I am thankful that I have weaknesses because this reminds me all the more of why I constantly NEED YOU! Your strength and love holds me together; sustains me. Your kindness fills me with joy to the point where no one and no circumstance can get me down. Thank you Lord! I love you!! ♡

33

STRESS

We are all well acquainted with stress. There are so many things in our life that cause us to be worried, pressured, and anxious. The world constantly presents us with unknowns and predicaments that steal our joy and rob our peace.

When we get in the presence of God and spend time in his Word, we are able to escape the stress of our lives and place our problems in his hands. God gives a peace that is unlike anything the world offers. He is focused on preparing us for his permanent kingdom, and, as a result, his presence offers hope and everlasting joy that is opposite to the trivial stressors of this life.

> *Those who love your instructions have great peace
> and do not stumble.*
>
> Psalm 119:165 NLT

Spend time in his presence today, letting his peace wash over your heart. Focus on his truth and his capability rather than your problems and incapacity. What is troubling you? God is able exchange it for peace that is beyond what you can imagine.

October 5, 2016

Today I woke up feeling achey and dehydrated. But now that I am fixing my eyes on Jesus all these things fade away. Lord I place all my worries and concerns in your hands. I choose to surrender and let you be God. Holy Spirit please come and guide me today. I trust you Lord and I love you. I choose to focus on your truth and your capability. Lord I ask that you would show me your love so that I can love others like you. Encourage others and pray for others like Jesus.

COMPARISON

In the age of social media, comparison has become an easier default for us than it's ever been before. When every image we see of others has been properly angled, edited, filtered, and cropped we are quickly led into the delusion that the lives we see portrayed in those images are perfect. We believe that the smiling faces we see in that post are always smiling, and the perfect homes with the beautiful lighting are permanently well-kept and polished.

The danger of these filtered images is that we end up comparing ourselves to something that isn't an accurate standard. What we don't see is the life outside that frame. We don't see the mess, the struggles, and the imperfections that are inevitably part of every life—even the perfect-looking ones.

> Let everyone be sure that he is doing his very best,
> for then he will have the personal satisfaction of work
> well done and won't need to compare himself with
> someone else.
>
> Galatians 6:4 TLB

God wants you to be so invested in the work that he has given you to do that you are not distracted or dissatisfied by what you see someone else doing. What does your unique lifestyle look like? Dive headfirst into it, saying yes to contentment and joy and moving forward into greater fulfillment and happiness.

October 9, 2016

I would say that my unique lifestyle would be that I love to invest and spend time with people. When I am open and lowly the Lord can use me. Allowing His Holy Spirit to take over gives me full freedom and confidence to walk in my sphere of grace. Although right now working as a Pharmacy Technician is not always relaxed or fun, it teaches me something new every day. I believe God has placed me here to shift the atmosphere and allow God to shine His light through and in me. Living with my grandma, kind, wise, and hospitable, has been some of the best time of my life. She has taught me so much and I wouldn't trade it for anything else. Right now I say, "Yes Lord! Yes to be content and yes to choosing joy. I say yes to moving forward with you Jesus into greater fulfillment and happiness. Amen!"

37

VULNERABILITY

Some of the most substantial and ultimately wonderful changes in our lives come from moments of vulnerability: laying our cards on the table, so to speak, and letting someone else know how much they really mean to us. But vulnerability takes one key ingredient: humility. And humility is not an easy pill to swallow.

Isn't it sometimes easier for us to pretend that conflict never happened than to face the fact that we made a mistake and wronged another person? It's not always easy to humble ourselves and fight for the resolution in an argument—especially when it means admitting our failures.

> He gives us more grace. That is why Scripture says:
> "God opposes the proud
> but shows favor to the humble."
>
> James 4:6 NIV

Who are you in the face of conflict? Do you avoid apologizing in an attempt to save face? Does your pride get in the way of vulnerability, or are you willing and ready to humble yourself for restoration in your relationships? God says that he will give favor and wisdom to the humble. What can you do today to humble yourself for the sake of a restored relationship?

October 9, 2016

Holy Spirit I invite you into my day. Have your way. Teach me humility and how to love people well. Show me how to be more vulnerable and sensitive to your voice. Thank you Holy Spirit for inviting me to come to you and release my hurt etc you and forgive that person that was trying to correct me. Thank you for teaching me to show grace, love, and mercy.

IMPOSSIBLE

What seems impossible to you today? What have you given up on, walked away from, and written off as absurd? What dreams have you let die simply because you felt they were unattainable?

Maybe our dreams, though they seem far off, were placed in our hearts for a purpose. And maybe they won't look exactly the way we always thought they would, but maybe they'll still come true in a new way. Maybe the things that seem insurmountable to us will be easily overcome when we simply shift perspective and look at them differently.

> *Behold, I will do a new thing,*
> *Now it shall spring forth;*
> *Shall you not know it?*
> *I will even make a road in the wilderness*
> *And rivers in the desert.*
>
> Isaiah 43:19 NKJV

Beloved, you serve a God who is powerful enough to make a path appear right through an empty wilderness and create a stream of life-giving water in the midst of a desert. He is more than able to take even the most impossible of situations and provide clarity, direction, and the means to make it through. Trust him with your impossibilities and rely on his strength for your weaknesses.

Thursday, October 13, 2016

Today nothing seems impossible with God. I have at times given up on Hillsong College or Bible College in general, but I hold tight to the loving, all-powerful, all-present, and all-knowing God. He has placed dreams like seeing people walk boldly for Jesus everyday in their work places, unashamed to reach out and pray for someone. To see women unite as a sisterhood championing one another and being there for each other, + doing life together for God's Kingdom. To see an awakening in high schoolers that they are all sons and daughters of the King, they have a purpose in God's kingdom, to get to know their true Heavenly Father, Holy Spirit friend and Helper, and how to walk with Jesus daily.

I have written off being a motivational speaker/ evangelist speaker as absurd, before. Or there have been times I wonder why I haven't become at least friends with my husband. But God! I trust you!

Redeem me! I will go. Send me! I will use me for your not mine.

You amaze me!

Have your way Lord!

FULLY ALIVE

Everyday living can suck the life right out of us. Somewhere in the middle of being stuck in traffic, sweeping floors, and brushing our teeth, we can forget to be alive.

What does it mean to be *alive*, rather than just to live? Not to only exist in life, but to know it, to understand it, to experience it—to *live* it. What would it be like? Freefalling from an airplane. Running through the grass barefoot with sun on your face. Bringing babies into the world, screaming and strong with power and life. What would it be like if we lived each moment in the spirit of those fully alive moments?

When you follow the revelation of the Word,
heaven's bliss fills your soul.

Proverbs 29:18 TPT

Without a reason for life, without purpose, we perish. We falter. We lose our way. We lose hope. We begin to casually exist instead of breathing in the reverence of a fully alive life. What dreams has God given you that you've lost along the way? Trust that they will be returned to you. God breathed life into you so that you could live it to the fullest.

Friday October 14, 2016
This morning I woke up and was not
feeling very well. But God is good! He
is with me! He is my joy! Blessed
is the women!! I choose to embrace
these aches I get or stuffy nose. I
choose to love God whole heartedly.
"Consider it pure joy, my brothers, whenever
you face trials of many kinds because you know
that the TESTING OF YOUR FAITH
DEVELOPS PERSEVERANCE."
~James 1:1-2
Lord thank you for these times. The times
I kept crying for no reason because they
drew me closer to you. Thank you for
bills because they remind me to trust and depend
on you. They remind me I am thankful to
be alive, sharing your love with others, and
that I have a mission every day besides a job.

43

A WAY OUT

Each of us struggles with temptation. No one is exempt. From gossip to overindulging, to unkind thoughts, and more, we battle with temptation in all different ways.

The good news is that we serve a God who is faithful, and, oh, how he loves his children! The Bible tells us that he won't allow us to be faced with more than what we can handle. When we turn to him in the midst of our struggles, we can find our way out.

> No temptation has overtaken you except what is common to mankind. And God is faithful; he will not let you be tempted beyond what you can bear. But when you are tempted, he will also provide a way out so that you can endure it.
>
> 1 Corinthians 10:13 NIV

Be prepared for your time of battle by praying for protection. Ask the Lord to open your eyes to see the ways in which you may fall, so that you can be ready to face them head on. Though temptation will surely come your way, be assured that it will not overcome you as you trust in the Lord.

Thursday November 17, 2016

This morning I am thankful for another day. Another day to live, love on others, encourage others, and adventure with Holy Spirit. I also am reminded to ask the Lord to open my eyes to see the ways in which I may fall, so that I can be ready to ~~face~~ them head on. The Lord told me to, "think before you speak. Listen intently and focus on me as you listen. Invite Holy Spirit, talk to Holy Spirit, and trust Holy Spirit. He has a lot of knowledge and loves to help.

HE HEARS

Sometimes it can feel as if God is far away: an elusive man in the heavens who is so far above us that surely he cannot be interested in our day-to-day lives. Our desires and requests seem so small by comparison that it seems unworthy a task to even ask him for help.

But he is a God who loves his children. He wants us to be happy, to feel fulfilled. When we approach him with our wants and needs, he truly hears us! The next time you feel as if your requests are too unimportant to bother God about, remind yourself that he is always listening. Though he may not answer you in the way you expect, he is right there beside you, ready to lend an ear.

This is the confidence we have in approaching God:
that if we ask anything according to his will, he hears us.
And if we know that he hears us—whatever we ask—we
know that we have what we asked of him.

1 John 5:14-15 NIV

Allow yourself to be filled with God's presence. He loves you and wants the best for you. What do you want from God today? If you ask in his will, he will answer you.

Monday October 17, 2016

Lord first off thank you for another day! I am blessed and grateful to be alive, here and now. Lord I come to you humbled and lowly in spirit asking for just You. All I really want is time with you. Lord I know you see my hurt and frustrations with work. But I know you heard me when I released them to you. Holy Spirit I need and want you! I need your counsel and guidance. You are so encouraging, loving, and kind. I want more joy. Overflowing with joy and zeal for you my Jesus. Take my life and let it be all for you Lord! I trust you and LOVE YOU! My best friend and my first and constant forever love! Lead me and I will follow You. "... Put your hope in God, for I will yet PRAISE HIM, MY SAVIOR and MY GOD."

47

-Psalm 42:5 (partial but important reminder)

REST SECURE

No matter where you are, God is there also. While there may be times when we ache to hide from him in our shame, he is a constant presence. The beautiful thing about his omnipresence is that we have a steady and consistent companion who is always ready to help in times of trouble.

We have no reason to fear the things that the world may throw our way. We've got the best protector of all at our side! Are you asking for his help in times of worry and woe, or are you turning inward to try to solve your problems?

> I keep my eyes always on the LORD.
> With him at my right hand, I will not be shaken.
> Therefore my heart is glad and my tongue rejoices;
> my body also will rest secure.
>
> Psalm 16:8-9 NIV

Let God be your refuge. Nothing is too big or too small for him! Even in your darkest hours, you can know true joy because he is your guardian. Take your cares and distress, and cast them upon him today because he can handle it. Rest secure in him.

"I AM COMPLETE IN HIM!"
-Colossians 2:10

Tuesday October 18, 2016

Today I am reminded of the Lord's new mercies every morning. I woke up feeling a bit tired, but I felt refreshed; renewed. Grateful all over again! Thankful to be alive, do life with Jesus, choosing joy, drinking a fresh hot cup of coffee, and getting in the Word.

I am also reminded to give, literally cast, all my cares and distress upon God today, because He can handle it. Lord right now I thank you for being in charge over and in my life. Thank you that you know what to do every second and you do it so clearly and in perfect timing. "Blessed is she who believed that the Lord would <u>fulfill</u> His promises to her."
- Luke 1:45

"Mightier then the waves of the sea is His love for you."
-Psalm 93:4

49

MELODY OF WORSHIP

Have you ever felt the song of your heart praising the Lord? No words may come, no verses, no chorus, and yet your very being feels as though it may burst from the music inside you. You are not alone! Even the very heavens praise him in this way!

The Bible tells us that without words, and without even the slightest sound, the skies burst forth in a song of praise for the glory of God. Isn't that an amazing picture? Can't you just envision an orchestra above you?

> God's splendor is a tale that is told;
> his testament is written in the stars.
> Space itself speaks his story every day
> through the marvels of the heavens.
> His truth is on tour in a starry-vault of the sky,
> showing his skill in creation's craftsmanship.
> Every day gushes out its message to the next,
> night with night whispering its knowledge to all.
> Without a sound, without a word, without a voice being heard,
> Yet all the world can see its story.
> Everywhere its gospel is clearly read so all may know.

Psalm 19:1-4 TPT

Break forth into your song! Allow your heart to feel the words, even if you cannot fully form them. Give God all your praises today. He is so deserving of them! Let your heart be a celebration of your love for Jesus Christ. Give in to the melody of worship inside you.

"Let the morning bring me word of
your unfailing love," - Psalm 143:8
for I have put my trust in you.
Show me the way I should go,
for to you I lift up my soul."

UNFAILING GOODNESS

Do you remember the first thing that you failed at? Maybe it was a test at school, a diet, a job interview, or even a relationship. Failure is difficult to admit, especially in a culture that values outward success and appearance. We often hear it said that success comes from many failures, but we only really hear that from successful people!

When Joshua was advanced in years, he reminded the Israelites of all that God had done for them. Though they had been unfaithful to God many times, God remained faithful, and they became a great nation that none could withstand.

> *"I am about to go the way of all the earth, and you know in your hearts and souls, all of you, that not one thing has failed of all the good things that the LORD your God promised concerning you; all have come to pass for you, not one of them has failed."*
>
> Joshua 23:14 NRSV

God had a plan and a purpose for the nation of Israel, and through his power and mercy he ensured that these plans succeeded. In the same way, God has a purpose for your life, and while you may fail, he will not. Take the opportunity today to submit your heart to his will. Know that not one good thing that God has planned for you will fail.

~ Wednesday October 26, 2016 ~

Lord thank you for being faithful 24/7!
Jesus, who am I to get to have
a relationship with you so intimately? Lord
you are so good and kind! Right now
I just humble myself before you Lord
and open up my hands in surrender and
say, "Come Holy Spirit. Lord I trust you and
I invite you to come into my heart, be
the Lord of my life, and have your way.
Let your will be done and not mine. Holy
Spirit breathe, move, and awaken in me whatever
you want. Thank you Lord for this
reminder that I have purpose and that
your promises will not fail. Lord I
say, "Yes! to walking with you every day,
dying to myself, carrying my cross, and
being led by Holy Spirit. I love you
God. I fear and reverence you. Come and breathe
within. I
also choose you let down all my walls. I give
you my past, present, and future. I want to
live for you every day. Amen.

53

ETERNAL FOUNTAINS

We take it for granted that when we turn on a faucet, water will come out. If we need something to drink, we can quench our thirst pretty easily. In Jesus' day, however, people (usually women) had to get their water from the well, often situated quite a walk away from their homes. It was a necessary daily task that provided for the family's needs.

Imagine then, being offered water that would last forever. This is what Jesus offered the woman at the well. She would never have to make this trip again in the heat of the day. She wanted this answer to her need. Jesus compared her desire with a spiritual desire: just as the well was a source for physical life, he was the source for eternal life.

> *"Whoever drinks of the water that I shall give him will never thirst. But the water that I shall give him will become in him a fountain of water springing up into everlasting life."*
>
> John 4:14 NKJV

You have received Jesus as the source for your life. Not only does Jesus say that he will provide you with everlasting water, but he says that this water will be like a fountain, springing up. Are you thankful for the eternal life that Jesus has placed within you? Remember to draw from him as your source of life today.

Sunday November 12, 2017

Lord I'm sorry. I repent of letting my circumstances authoritate my life, thoughts, decisions, perspective, focus, ideas, etc. I am struggling Lord with being content. I am feeling like I am a small brook or spring rather than a fountain spring up with joy. Lord I choose you right now, I choose you as my source of life to draw from. I lay down everything at your feet, and say, I love you, trust you, believe in you, depend on you, put my hope in you, want to serve and follow you. I open up my heart to you Lord. Come and have your way. I love you God

THE WORD

We are met with a lot of opposition in our daily pursuit of Christ. We get sidetracked so easily with the things of this world, our own emotional struggles, and our war with sin. Without the truth of the living, active Word of God, we are defenseless to successfully live the Christian life.

The Word of God is our best defense against hopelessness, fear, and sin—and at the same time it's our best offensive weapon against temptation, lies, and the enemy of our souls.

How can a young man keep his way pure?
By guarding it according to your word.
With my whole heart I seek you;
let me not wander from your commandments!
I have stored up your word in my heart,
that I might not sin against you.

Psalm 119:9-11 ESV

Make a goal for yourself to memorize Scripture that will equip you for daily living. Write verses in your journal, hang them on your refrigerator, and frame them on your walls. The Word of God is the most useful, instructive, powerful book that you will ever get your hands on. Eat it, absorb it, know it, and live it.

○ Sunday December 3, 2017 ○
How can a young man keep his way
pure? By guarding it according to your
word. With my whole heart I
seek you; let me not wander
from your Commandments! I have
stored up your word in my heart,
that I might not sin against you.
Psalm 119:9-11 ESV

BUSYNESS

Our lives are so full that we often have difficulty finding time to spend with Jesus. We have so much that demands our attention, it can be hard to find time to consecrate a portion of our day to God.

God, who has existed for eternity, is not bound by time. Because he is outside of time, time does not limit him the way that it limits us. When we take even a few sacred minutes to spend in his presence in the midst of our busy day, he can meet us there and download deep truths to our hearts.

"Come away by yourselves to a secluded place and rest a while." (For there were many people coming and going, and they did not even have time to eat.)

Mark 6:31 NASB

In the days when you feel you don't even have time to eat, ask God to give you the grace to find a few moments to slip away alone in his presence. God will speak volumes to a heart that is open to his truth—even over the hustle and bustle of your busiest days.

Lord, ♡

I love you.
Show me how to love like
you have loved me.

LIVING WORD

Have you ever noticed God speaking to you in themes? We all go through different seasons in life, and God speaks to our hearts accordingly. Some of us may be going through a season of learning to wait, while another is learning how to step out in faith. But the beautiful thing about God is that he is big enough to speak to all of us—in our different places, with our different hearts—at the same time, with the same words.

God's Word is alive and active. It can deliver truth to the heart of each unique person. Two people can get something completely different from the same passage of Scripture because of what God has been doing in each of their hearts separately. Through the body of Christ, we can come together and share what God is teaching us—multiplying our individual growth as we encourage one another.

> The word of God is living and active and sharper than any two-edged sword, and piercing as far as the division of soul and spirit, of both joints and marrow, and able to judge the thoughts and intentions of the heart.
>
> Hebrews 4:12 NASB

Never doubt the power of what you hold in your hands when you read the Word of God. Your Creator knows you so intimately because he is the one who handcrafted your soul— and he cares about you enough to speak directly to your heart through his living Word. What is he speaking to you today?

Totes me right now! 12/4/17

Monday December 4, 2017

I have noticed I am more patient with people and their timing than I am with God and His timing. Yikes! Lord I repent of putting people before you. I repent of being forgetful, lazy, condemning to myself, and for being aware of Your constant presence. Father I ask for your help. I want You to be the Lord over every part of my life. I want You to be the King of my heart. ♡ I want to be led by Your voice, Your Holy Spirit. Remind me to be bold and brave by stepping out of in faith every. single. day! Refresh my mind of the last thing you told me to do, dream, to speak, to pray for, and what is on your heart right now that I can speak and desire as well.

UNCOMPLICATED FREEDOM

We over-complicate freedom in the Christian life. Through our legalisms, we try to find a way to humanize the redeeming work of the cross because we simply can't wrap our minds around the supernatural character of God.

It can be hard to understand the complete grace offered at Calvary because we are incapable of giving that kind of grace. But when God says that he has forgotten our sin, and that he has made us new, he really means it. God is love, and love keeps no record of wrongs. Nothing can keep us from his love. Salvation tore the veil that separated us from the holiness of God. That complete work cannot be diminished or erased by anything we do.

> *I have swept away your offenses like a cloud,*
> *your sins like the morning mist.*
> *Return to me,*
> *for I have redeemed you.*
>
> Isaiah 44:22 NIV

Freedom is truly that simple. The beauty of the Gospel can be summed up in this single concept—grace, though undeserved, given without restraint. Can you accept it today?

MY THOUGHTS

....

....

....

....

....

....

....

....

....

....

....

....

....

....

....

....

....

SAND CASTLES

Have you ever been sitting on a beach and watched a little child work tirelessly on an elaborate sand castle? They spend hours perfecting their creation, thoughtfully forming each section, often stepping back to admire their work. But these little children are unaware of the patterns of ocean waves and don't realize that as the day passes, their masterpieces will eventually be swept away by the swelling tide. All that work, all that concentration, all that pride, gone as the water erases the shore.

What proverbial castles are we building in our lives that could, at any moment, be simply erased? We've got to buy into the bigger vision. We must know what can last and what won't. There are temporary kingdoms and a kingdom that will never pass away. We have to recognize which one we are contributing to.

> *"Don't store up treasures here on earth where they can erode away or may be stolen. Store them in heaven where they will never lose their value and are safe from thieves. If your profits are in heaven, your heart will be there too."*

Matthew 6:19-21 TLB

If your work and your heart are invested in a heavenly vision, then what you have spent your life on will continue to matter for longer than you live. Spend your time investing in the eternal souls of people, in the eternal vision of advancing God's kingdom, and in the never-ending truth of the Gospel. In these things you will find purpose and treasure that will never be lost. Where is your treasure today?

Monday December 5, 2016

Where is your treasure today?

That's a great question because lately I have felt ~~money~~ unprioritized with my finances. I have been carrying around or storing up cash in the wrong places. I can't even remember the last time I tithed. I haven't been to church in 3 weeks and I haven't served in the youth since the retreat. But the Holy Spirit just whispered to me, "God still loves you." Repent, ask for forgiveness, and move on. Lord right now I repent of lying, being lazy, worried about my health, and defensive. I ask Holy Spirit to come and convict me of these sins more often. I ask Lord for your forgiveness and grace. Help me Jesus to lean into you and trust you. I choose to put all my hope, love, trust, and heart (treasure) in You.

THE SPICE RACK

Anyone who does any amount of cooking has a spice rack—that one place where all seasonings are kept within easy reach of the stovetop. There are some spices that get used consistently: garlic, salt, and pepper. And there are other spices that may only be used once in a while: cardamom, tarragon, anise. While those lesser-used spices may collect dust in the back of our spice cupboards, we still rely on them to bring out just the right flavor in that one particular meal.

Life is a lot like a spice rack. We shelve our experiences like spices: some make so much sense—like salt and pepper—we pull from them often, clearly recognizing their usefulness. Other experiences are more subtle and undeclared; sometimes we go years never understanding why we had them. But then, in one moment, our life recipe will call for a little saffron. And all at once, it will make so much sense. That experience we had—the one we thought we must've had by mistake—will be the only one that matters for that moment.

> *We know that in everything God works for the good of those who love him. They are the people he called, because that was his plan.*
>
> Romans 8:28 NCV

Is there a season in your life that you often wonder about. You might look at that time and only see failure or waste. When you can't make sense of why it happened, remember that God will work it *all* for his good because you love him.

~ Tuesday December 20, 2016 ~

The season that I am currently in has me wondering very often. Like what was causing my health to have trouble swallowing? Is there something seriously wrong with my body? How can I get healthier? I don't want to be more stress for my grandma and family. But God you are so good and faithful. And though I am choosing grace and peace over logic, I trust you. I know you are here with me inside me even. Holy Spirit help! I need you and want you to pour oil on my fire inside for you. I love you Jesus. May this season as well as all my other seasons bring you glory God.

"Every good and perfect gift is from above, coming down from the Father of the heavenly lights, who does not change like shifting shadows. He chose to give us birth through the word of truth,

SUSTAINED

There is always something to worry about, isn't there? Whether health, finances, relationships, or details, there are many unknowns in life that can easily keep us worrying. But what if we stopped worrying? What if we stopped questioning and decided instead to feel peace? What if we could trust completely that God would take care of us and our loved ones. God is our rock and he alone will sustain us.

The words in Psalm 3 can bring us comfort and peace when we are fearful. It speaks volumes about the grace of God: the protection and safety of his hand. But the verse goes beyond peace and comfort to the power of God. We only wake up because of his sustaining power. When we trust and believe in this God who possesses the power of life and death, what do we have to fear? Our entire lives are in his hands. We can't change that fact, so we might as well rest in it.

Lord, I trust in you. 7/14/17

I lay down and slept; I awoke, for the Lord sustains me.

Psalm 3:5 NASB

Thank you Papa Daddy for never letting go. 7/14/17

There will be many unknowns in your life. There will be moments when the rug feels as though it's been pulled out from under you, and there is nothing to do but despair. In those moments that you can't control, you *can* trust. What are you worried about right now? You can rest your soul, your mind, and your body in the hands of the one who has the power to sustain you.

68

Yes Lord. Thank you 7/14/17 Lord.

~ Friday night July 14, 2017 ~
Wow. Was this devotional ever right on target
with my life right now. Specifically my health.
There are quite some unknowns, unanswered
questions, and worries. But I choose right now
to say thank you Lord that you know and for
your constant faithfulness and companionship
through it all. I choose to lay all unknowns, uncertainties,
worries, anxieties, questions, frustrations, fears, + stress
at your feet. I'm letting go of what is not meant
for me to carry. And I am choosing to trust you
Jesus. I am choosing to lean into you and hold
onto your hand. Your warm embrace. Your steadfast
love. Your promises. I choose to trust in
You. I fix my eyes on you. I open myself
to you to receiving your love, peace, joy, grace,
and healing.
Holy Spirit lead me to where I should go
next. Show me what foods to eat, what to drink
and help me to swallow better + not choke.

STUMBLING IN THE DARK

Have you ever walked somewhere in the pitch black? You bump into things, knock stuff over, and often can't even place where you are or where you're going. Everything becomes muddled in the darkness. Without light to guide us, we can't see where we're going, or what we're running into.

Many times throughout the Bible, God likens being in sin to being in darkness. When we immerse ourselves in sin, thus rejecting the light of the truth, we can no longer see what we are running into. The darkness will cloud our thinking and our rationale, and we won't even be able to determine what sins are coming our way. By allowing sinful messages to enter our souls through different avenues, we lose our ability to navigate our lives.

The Word gave life to everything that was created,
and his life brought light to everyone.
The light shines in the darkness,
and the darkness can never extinguish it.

John 1:4-5 NLT

When wickedness begins to overtake your life, you lose the ability to recognize what is making you sin. Strive to keep your soul sensitive to the truth. Keep sight of the light by spending time in God's Word.

Friday December 23, 2016

♡♡First off, GOD IS SO GOOD!!!!♡♡♡♡
He has healed me from not being able
to swallow to swallowing easily. Thank
you Lord for you love, grace, kindness,
faithfulness, trustworthiness, healing, and
truth. Thank you Jesus for
giving me freedom, a relationship
with you, and hope. I love you Papa
Daddy. I repent of worrying, doubting,
stressing, getting anxious, and questioning you.
I ask for your grace and forgiveness
Jesus! Thank you for peace too. ♡
Next thought: Immersion ~ This word caught
me off guard, in a good way. Am I immersed
in Jesus? Holy Spirit? The healthy things over
hostile and harmful things? When you're immersed
you are ALL IN! Completely drenched
and in over your head. I choose to
be immersed in you, Jesus! Immersed
fully in your fine Holy Spirit!

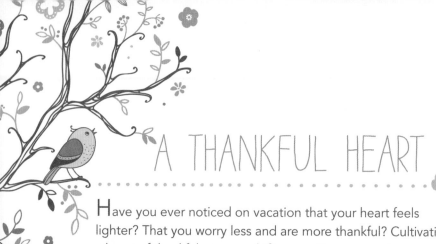

A THANKFUL HEART

Have you ever noticed on vacation that your heart feels lighter? That you worry less and are more thankful? Cultivating a heart of thankfulness can shift our entire perspective on life. When we are grateful, we start to see the light of God so much more. We start to see him *everywhere*.

A thankful heart is a heart that refuses to let the enemy in and deceive us. Suddenly, our circumstances seem not so terrible, our problems not so huge. A heart of gratitude glorifies God and keeps us centered on him. Just like on vacation, you can have that same perspective every day—even in the most mundane circumstances.

> *Whatever you do, whether in word or deed, do it all in the name of the Lord Jesus, giving thanks to God the Father through him.*
>
> Colossians 3:17 NIV

What can you do to start cultivating a heart of gratitude? A heart of thankfulness keeps you grounded in Christ, in communion with him, and allows you to live the fullest life he's designed for you.

Merry Christmas!
December 25, 2016.

One way I can keep a heart of gratitude is by having a heart of repentance. This keeps my soul in check with the Lord and allows the Holy Spirit to breathe and move in me. Jesus right now I just thank you for another day. Thank you for this devotional reminder to stay grateful. Thank you for family, good health getting better, friends, clothing, a home, food, and freedom. Ultimately, thank you Jesus for You! Thank you for giving me the best life I could ever ask for. I will praise you through good and bad times. I love you Lord! Have your way in me! Holy Spirit come and fill me up and breathe in me. I love you!!

73

HEART CENTER

Social media: an escape, a gift, a communicative tool, a joy stealer, a comparison thief, a comedian, entertainment. Social media can be fun! But it can also become an idol when we don't recognize it as such. Suddenly, instead of opening up our Bible, we are clicking on our phones checking Facebook, posting photos and status updates to seek attention and approval from people rather than our Creator.

God's desire for our life is that we chose him above all else. He wants to be our focal point, one we return to time and again, so we don't ever steer too far off course. Instead of seeking approval from others, let's turn our eyes toward the one who loves us most, whose voice is the only one we should hear.

> *If then you have been raised with Christ, seek the things that are above, where Christ is, seated at the right hand of God. Set your minds on things that are above, not on things that are on earth.*
>
> Colossians 3:1-2 ESV

Where do you choose to spend the majority of your time? What choices could you eliminate to stay centered on Jesus? In a busy life of choices, it's important to know your back-up is also your best option—seeking God and choosing life with him.

MY THOUGHTS

THE VOICE
OF LOVE

When we live for other voices, we will quickly become worn out and discouraged. Other people's expectations for how we should live, act, and be are sometimes unreachable. There is one voice that matters, and it can come in a variety of forms—the voice of God.

What God would tell us is that we are loved, we are cherished, and we have significant value. We are his beloved, his daughters, his beautiful creation. This is the voice that matters. This is the voice to come back to when we feel like we're not enough.

> "The Father gives me the people who are mine.
> Every one of them will come to me,
> and I will always accept them."
>
> John 6:37 NCV

What are the voices you typically listen to? Can you ignore them and focus only on the voice that matters? He will encourage you and remind you that you *are* enough. Nothing you do or don't do is going to make him love you any more or any less. Soak it in, so you can drown out all the other voices.

Tuesday December 27, 2016

Good morning my beloved Jesus. I thank you Lord for another great day. Lord lately I have been sad and scared about my health. I don't have any idea what's going on, but you do. And that's the best place for the answers to be. Lord help me to silent out all other voices so I can clearly hear yours. Pappa Daddy I love you so so so so much's I know that you love me abundantly, vastly, much much more. Help me Jesus to be a sponge soaking up your voice and encouragement. Teach me to trust you more to hope in you more. To love you more. Holy Spirit come and cover me in light. Teach me how to build up a well of peace and joy. Wherever I go I know you are with me. Lead me lord, I trust you and love you and want to follow you all the days of my life.

77

BREAK EVERY CHAIN

There is a chance to start over—every day if we need to. From the inside out, we can be transformed and our hearts renewed. We can essentially remake ourselves with the help, healing, and transformative nature of Christ! Jesus died on the cross to promise us a life free from the bondage of sin, free from hopelessness, free from any chains that try to trap us. In Christ, we are set free.

We need to hear the truth of Christ's promise for us and stop the cycle of hopelessness, defeat, and bondage to sin. All we need to do is get on our knees and pray.

> *"His purpose in all of this is that they should seek after God, and perhaps feel their way toward him and find him—though he is not far from any one of us."*
>
> Acts 17:27 TLB

Is there an area of your life that you need to receive freedom from? Wait for God's voice to permeate the deepest, saddest parts of you. He wants you to let him take care of you. He is pursuing your heart.

Thursday December 29, 2016

12/28 Last night the Lord gave me a crazy revelation when I was crying because I was so hungry. I said out loud, "So this is what people in 3rd world countries feel like. It's probably way worse but I get to experience that last night." Then the Holy Spirit said, "Think about this hunger on a spiritual level. Many people are hungry, desperately hungry for Jesus and they go around starving themselves. Your soul is the most important part of your being.

12/29 An area of my life I need to receive freedom is worry. Worry about my health. Lord I surrender to you again. Allowing you to come into my heart, to let you take care of me, and to let you pursue my heart. I love you Papa Daddy. ♡

GLORIOUS

Leaves changing from green to orange to red. Gently falling snow. A rainbow-colored sunrise. A sprout of newness in the dirt. The smell of freshly cut grass. The rustling of leaves in the trees. The smell of a pine tree at Christmas time. Billowy, moving clouds. Sunshine kissing your cheeks. It is amazing that our Creator would make all of this for us to enjoy. It's glorious, really.

Yet, days can go by and we haven't stopped to notice. We forget to slow down. We ignore this incredibly beautiful world that he made for us to explore and enjoy. It is amazing what a walk with a friend, a run through the woods, or the feel of bare feet on grass can do for our soul.

> *On the glorious splendor of your majesty,*
> *and on your wondrous works, I will meditate.*
>
> Psalm 145:5 NRSV

Do you take time to get outside and enjoy all that he created? The next time you're feeling a bit squirmy, slow down, take a walk outside, and soak in his presence that's all around you: in the grass between your toes, in the rustle of leaves above you, and in the sunshine kissing your cheeks.

Tuesday January 17, 2017

With it being winter I don't go outside that much. I do however, sit by a window or just glean out one and look at the beauty all around me. I choose to be in awe and wonder of all that He created. Looking out my window upstairs it appears gloomy but yet still glorious. There is such an amazing stillness in the trees and a steadiness in the way the branches are pointed upward. They have a steadfast posture of their heart almost. They worship and show adoration to their Creator. The fog makes it clearer to see things around you rather then looking to far ahead. So this is what it's like to sit, be still, and know that He is God. ♡

TRUST IN THE LITTLE THINGS

God has given us a huge gift in his faithful nature. He promises us things and sticks to those promises without fail.

It feels easier to trust God in the big moments, the desperate moments. But what about the everyday moments? The times that we grab hold of control and want to do it all ourselves. In those moments, we can press into him without restraint. Let go, cry out to him, ask him to carry you. And he will. The everyday moments that might feel crooked will be straightened. He will carry you as he promises.

Those who know Your name will put their trust in You;
For You, LORD, have not forsaken those who seek You.

Psalm 9:10 NKJV

How beautiful is this God! He will give you a path to confidently walk on if all you do is trust him. Where do you have the most difficulty trusting God? Practice letting go in those moments. Trust him.

MY THOUGHTS

....

....

....

....

....

....

....

....

....

....

....

....

....

....

....

....

GOD'S EAR

God hears you. Whether you are shouting praises of thanksgiving, crying tears of mourning, or singing phrases of glory, God hears. He listens. He does not abandon or ignore.

He hears your voice. He hears your heart. He hears your shouts, your whispers, and your thoughts. Sometimes this seems scary; we feel like we have to perform. That is a lie. Do not believe it. God takes us as we are, where we are. We don't have to filter, pretend, or please. He meets us, loves us, accepts us just as we are in this moment.

> I love the Lord, for he heard my voice;
> he heard my cry for mercy.
> Because he turned his ear to me,
> I will call on him as long as I live…
> Then I called on the name of the Lord:
> "Lord, save me!"
> The Lord is gracious and righteous;
> our God is full of compassion.
> The Lord protects the unwary;
> when I was brought low, he saved me.
> Return to your rest, my soul,
> for the Lord has been good to you.
>
> Psalm 116: 1-7 NIV

Do you believe God hears you? What do you want to tell him right now? He is a beautiful, caring God who takes us as sinners and holds our hand as we walk the path to salvation.

MY THOUGHTS

REST IN JESUS

Have you ever been awake when you think no one else is? Maybe you had an early morning flight, and you feel you are the only person who could possibly be stirring at that hour. It feels kind of magical, doesn't it? It's like you have an unshared secret. Regardless of you being a night owl, morning person, or somewhere in-between, there is peace that comes with meeting Jesus in secret—when your world has stopped for a bit.

Whatever it looks like, rising early or staying up late, taking a work break, a study break, or a mommy break, finding that quiet is where you can actually acquire strength. We need spiritual food to conquer each day.

> *He who dwells in the secret place of the Most High*
> *Shall abide under the shadow of the Almighty.*
>
> Psalm 91:1 NKJV

Can you find daily quiet time to meet with Jesus? He will meet you in that space, filling you with peace, strength, and love to go out and conquer the world.

~ Tuesday January 31, 2017 ~

Sitting here in an oil change car shoppe I am reminded that we all need to sit down and get our own oil changed. Spiritually we need more annointed oil from Jesus. He says in His Word, "Come to me all who are weary and heavy burdened and I will give you rest." You can't run a car without oil. Just like you yourself can't survive without Jesus and His Holy Spirit. The body needs fuel too such as water, nutrition, and exercise. But the soul is the most important. So be intentional on getting, literally making time for Jesus just for Him. TO be with Him. TO (or see what moves their heart. be like him. You can't learn To be like someone if you never make time for them.

CHANGE
OF SEASON

You will, undoubtedly, have various seasons in your life: seasons of longing and contentment, seasons of discouragement and joy, seasons of more and less. Being a grown-up means stretching into new ways of living, and this usually doesn't happen until the season hits.

Seasons can be challenging. They require bravery, obedience, dedication, and sometimes total upheaval of everything comfortable in our lives. If we feel that impending corner of a season change in our hearts, it usually means God is preparing us for something different—a *change*. In those seasons of life, the one who won't change, won't back down, and won't leave us stranded is our heavenly Father.

> *"Be strong and courageous, and act; do not fear nor be dismayed, for the LORD God, my God, is with you. He will not fail you nor forsake you until all the work for the service of the house of the LORD is finished."*
>
> 1 Chronicles 28:20 NASB

Do you see an impending season change approaching? How does it make you feel? Be brave! God will not move you into something without giving you the grace you need to make it through.

MY THOUGHTS

PEACE
LIKE A RIVER

Where do you usually go to find peace? Is there a certain place? A certain person? One of the greatest gifts of God is his undeniable, unfathomable peace. It is a deep well that comes with knowing and experiencing Jesus' love. No matter where we are, where we are going, and whatever we might be experiencing, his peace is greater.

Grasp how deep his well runs. Lasting peace and joy does not come in the world or people around you. Although those can be comforting, true, transforming, and powerful peace can only come from our Father. And oh, how he loves when we come to his well.

> *"I am the LORD your God,*
> *who teaches you what is best for you,*
> *who directs you in the way you should go*
> *…your peace would have been like a river,*
> *your well-being like the waves of the sea."*
>
> Isaiah 48:17-18 NIV

Where do you usually turn for peace? Have you experienced the indescribable peace of God?

MY THOUGHTS

JOYOUS JOURNEY

There is great joy in the journey: in the mundane details, in the difficult times, in the confusing moments, and in the tears. There is so much joy to be found in the quiet and in the noise.

Pity parties and comparisons create a direct path for the enemy to steal our joy. There is hope in Jesus and the gift of little joy-filled moments. They come in varying forms: sunshine rays pouring in the windows, a nice person at the check-out counter, a turn-the-radio-as-high-as-it-can-go kind of song, a dance party in the living room, or the taste of a delicious meal after a long day. Whatever the moment, there is joy if we look for it.

> *Consider it pure joy, my brothers and sisters, whenever you face trials of many kinds, because you know that the testing of your faith produces perseverance. Let perseverance finish its work so that you may be mature and complete, not lacking anything.*
>
> James 1:2-4 NIV

There's a journey of joy in waking up every day knowing it's another day to breathe in the fresh air, head to dinner with a girlfriend, or grab coffee with a co-worker. Find joy in the moment.

Thursday February 2, 2017

Today is a new day. A new day for opportunities, lessons, teaching, learning, listening, laughing, experiencing, and so much more. "This is the day that the Lord has made. I will REJOICE and be GLAD in it" - Psalm 118:24 What a great and vital reminder! There is joy in each moment, we just have to choose it. Sitting here in the Otsego Public Library on this cold and slippery day I am reminded of how I have so many books at home. Books about love, revival, hope, and kindness. I need to be more intentional about reading. And on a side note cleaning. Thank you Jesus for these simple realizations. You are so, so good! ♥

THE RACE

We are running this race to win a prize that is far greater than we could ever know. Our Lord was obedient until death with what he was meant to do. However, he did grow overwhelmed and three times asked his father if there was another way (see Luke 22). Jesus persevered with the help of angels.

There will be times when you feel like you are slipping and times when you'll fall, but be assured, Jesus will pick you up. Continue to move forward with a steadfast heart and a desire to persevere until you have finished your race.

> *Blessed is the one who perseveres under trial because, having stood the test, that person will receive the crown of life that the Lord has promised to those who love him.*
>
> James 1:12 NIV

Have there been times on your spiritual walk where you have wanted to give up? Let Jesus pick you back up and help you get back on track.

Saturday, February 4, 2017
    Jesus first off I love you.
Thank you for helping me and
carrying me when I wanted to
stay down.

HE KNOWS WHEN WE DON'T

You stare at the menu, overwhelmed by choices. Pasta sounds yummy, but you're avoiding gluten. Salad sounds healthy, but you just had that for lunch. Steak sounds perfect until you look at the price. Everyone else has ordered; all eyes are on you. You know you're hungry, just not what *for*. "What do I want?" you ask, though not expecting an answer.

There are days prayer can feel like that. We know we want something—we sense an ache or longing—but can't quite identify it. Other times, we're simply in too much pain to focus. We need, we need… but we can't get the words out. "What do I want?" we cry. This time, we *can* expect an answer. The Holy Spirit, because he lives inside us, knows us so intimately he can actually step in and pray on our behalf. He knows, even when we don't.

> *The Spirit helps us with our weakness. We do not know how to pray as we should. But the Spirit himself speaks to God for us, even begs God for us with deep feelings that words cannot explain.*
>
> Romans 8:26 NCV

Spend some time with the Spirit today. Thank him for knowing your heart, and sharing it with God when you can't.

Saturday, April 8, 2017

Sitting in an angled parking spot in St. Joe thinking about how good God is. Holy Spirit thank you for knowing me and my heart. Thank you for sharing my heart with God even when I can't. Thank you Holy Spirit for a relationship with you and through Jesus to the Father. I hear Holy Spirit asking, "Will you trust me to take you places farther than you ever thought you would go in order to share the gospel?" "I say Yes Lord! I trust you!!" "Will you trust me to provide the funds if I ask you to raise support for my ministry?" "Yes Lord I trust you with my finances!" "Will you trust me to bring you your husband that will be so in love with me and go-hand-in-hand with you for my kingdom in my perfect timing?" "Yes Lord! It's like you read my mind and heart."

BEING KNOWN

Think of the most perfect gift you've ever received. Not the most extravagant, but the one that was just so perfectly *you* that you realized the giver really knew you. They heard you, that one time, when you mentioned that one thing, perhaps in passing, and because they were listening with their heart, they saw into yours. They get you.

We love to be understood, and long to be seen. For many of us it's how we know we are loved. How much, then, must the Father love us? He who knows everything about us—who takes the time to listen to every longing and comfort every sigh—is waiting to give us his perfect gifts. We are known. We are loved.

> *You know what I long for, LORD;*
> *you hear my every sigh.*
>
> Psalm 38:9 NLT

Share your longing with God today. Let him show you his great love by revealing how intimately he knows you. Let him give you a good and perfect gift.

April 10, 2017

Father I long to be healed from this hesitation with swallowing and coughing up flem from dairy and certain foods. I choose to have faith in you Lord for healing. I trust you and love you Papa Daddy God.

April 11, 2017

Good morning Papa Daddy and Holy Spirit! I love you both so much! I am enjoying your presence on my later work day. Thank you Lord for the peace and intimacy. I am getting filled up even more than I could ever imagine. During this time together Lord I ask that you would show me what it is you are calling me to do. What gifts and talents that you have given me, can be used for what you are calling me to do?

IN TIMES OF DOUBT

The sun will set tonight; it will rise tomorrow. This is truth. We have no reason to doubt what we've witnessed every day of our lives. But when experience tells us otherwise, or perhaps we have no experience to go on, doubts creep in. It's going to snow tomorrow. "I doubt that," we say.

When someone we trust says they'll be there for us, we have faith in their words. Someone who has repeatedly let us down can make the same promise, but we remain uncertain until they've shown up and proven themselves. We're unsettled. We doubt. God wants to erase our doubt and he will; we only need to have faith.

> *God you are near me always, so close to me;*
> *every one of your commands reveals truth.*
> *I've known all along how true and unchanging*
> *is every word you speak, established forever!*

Psalm 119:151-152 TPT

Examine your prayer life. Do you trust God, or do you doubt his promises to you? Why? Share your heart openly with him, and ask him for unwavering faith.

Father right now I repent of doubting and questioning and worrying about the plans you have for me and my family. Lord I ask for your grace and forgiveness. Holy Spirit help me to turn to you for unwavering faith and for guidance and direction. I want to know you more Holy Spirit, Father, and Jesus. Reveal yourself to me Jesus. ♡ I love yo

April 11, 2017 Cont.

"You have a gift with making people feel loved and valued. You have a strength through me for compassion and justice. You long to see people fall in love with Me Jesus and come together in love and unity. You are a carrier of joy and the Gospel. You have great humility and a rare but beautiful meekness through Holy Spirit. You also have a huge caring heart. You have grit and boldness. You exemplify my love Allison. The more you spend time with me, the better love you have for people. The more grace you get to give and show people and yourself. How would you like to pioneer a youth movement in the midwest? You can create different houses for youth to stay + pay cheap rent while they are in school, working, volunteering, in between seasons, etc. and there can be worship, a prayer room, a weekly community event, get connected with missions, a church, Host revival events, support raise.

PLEASE REMAIN SEATED

When riding in a moving car, boat, or plane, we wouldn't just jump out, no matter how restless or impatient we were feeling. That would be crazy. We couldn't possibly expect to arrive at our destination as safely or as quickly—or perhaps at all. We grasp the necessity of remaining where we are if we are to get where we are going.

Why, then, are we so quick to jump ahead when it comes to God's plans for our lives? We accept his grace, but not his timing. We welcome his comfort, but not his discipline. How often do we decide without praying, or act without his prompting? And yet we expect to get where we are going—safely, quickly, easily.

> *"Remain in me, as I also remain in you. No branch can bear fruit by itself; it must remain in the vine. Neither can you bear fruit unless you remain in me."*
>
> John 15:4 NIV

Are there areas of your life you are trying to direct on your own? Spend some time praying for the Spirit to reveal to you anywhere you are not abiding in Jesus, or trusting his timing. Ask him to help you trust him.

8:41pm

Saturday, April 15, 2017
What a beautiful day today was! Jesus you spoil me! This devotional is deep, but definitely needed. There are many areas of my life I am trying to direct on my own. My future career-wise, my health, finances, family, love life, passions, my faith, friendships, balance with life, etc. because society tells us we need to "get it together or have everything figured out for the next 20 years. When Jesus is the exact opposite, is way simpler, and designed it all. Jesus came so that you and me can have life and have life abundantly. Jesus also said not to worry but rather trust Him. He also said we're not promised tomorrow. Holy Spirit I ask that you would reveal to me any where I am not abiding in Jesus or trusting his timing. I ask you Holy Spirit, please help me to trust him.

103

TRUST THE LIGHT

Imagine yourself in total darkness, perhaps a wilderness camping trip (or a power failure at a nice hotel if that's more your speed). It's the middle of the night, and you must find your way back to camp. Turn on your flashlight. Though it only illuminates a few steps at a time, it's enough to keep moving. Each step forward lights more of the way, and eventually, you see your destination.

Our faith walk is very much like this. Most of the time, we can't see where we're headed. Although just a few steps ahead is all we can make out for certain, we trust the path the light reveals.

"I am the Light of the world; he who follows Me will not walk in the darkness, but will have the Light of life."

John 8:12 NASB

Jesus is our light. He shows us just what we need to see to put one foot forward at a time. Ask him to help you ignore the unseen and trust the light.

MY THOUGHTS

OUR COMFORTER

It's the end of a long, difficult day. All you want to do is crawl in bed, wrap up in your comforter, and rest. Something about a soft, fluffy blanket helps problems seem less like problems.

One of God's many names is the *God of all comfort*. He is our ultimate comforter, allowing us to wrap ourselves in him and be warmed, reassured, and relieved. He does this so we can pay it forward, wrapping ourselves around others in need of comfort, and showing them his love.

> *Praise be to the God and Father of our Lord Jesus Christ, the Father of compassion and the God of all comfort, who comforts us in all our troubles, so that we can comfort those in any trouble with the comfort we ourselves receive from God.*
>
> 2 Corinthians 1:3-4 NIV

Notice the repetition in the verses above. The word *comfort* appears four times. This isn't because Paul was feeling uninspired; it's because he wanted to make sure we heard him. We are comforted so that we can comfort. God wants both for us. Which have you done more of lately? Ask him to help you with the other.

4/

DO EVERYTHING IN LOVE

What goes through your mind as you shop for groceries? How about during your workouts? While you read, or watch TV, do your thoughts turn to love? As you do dishes, is there love in the way you rinse a glass, or as you dry a pot?

First Corinthians contains the rather extraordinary command to do everything in love. *Everything.* What would that look like? How does one pick lovingly through packages of strawberries, searching for the reddest, juiciest ones? Is there a loving way to scrub the broiler pan? Perhaps not, but we most certainly can approach our daily lives in a state of love, filled with it, thereby assuring all we do will be done in love.

Do everything in love.

1 Corinthians 16:14 NCV

Rather than consider how to bring more love to your activities, pray today asking to be filled to the brim with love. From there, simply let it flow.

~ Tuesday, May 16, 2017 ~
Good morning Jesus and Holy Spirit!
What a great reminder:
— DO EVERYTHING IN LOVE. —
1 Corinthians 16:14
Lord I surrender myself to you.
Please come and reveal yourself to me.
Fill me up to the brim with your
love. Deepen ^sweeten ^pour love, compassion, kindness,
grace, humility, and joy for people in me. Lord
I want to ultimately deepen my love, reverence, intimacy,
adoration, fervent prayers, and awe for you.
Holy Spirit I ask that you would prune
the insecurities, doubts, negative thoughts/words/actions,
defenses, offenses, misinterpretations, fears, worries, anxieties,
hurts, lies, accusations, and fakeness out of my mind
and heart. I ask that you, Holy Spirit would
birth in me a greater love, faith, grace, compassion, peace,
humility, and joy in the deepest depths of my
heart. Then, LET IT FLOW to those around
me. Thank you Lord for another day. Amen.

FINDING PEACE

What does chaos look like in your world? Crazy work deadlines, over-scheduled activities, long to-do lists and short hours? All of the above? How about peace? What does that look like?

Most of us immediately picture having gotten away, whether to the master bathroom tub or a sunny beach. It's quiet. Serene. The trouble with that image, lovely as it is, is that it's fleeting. We can't live in our bathtubs or in Fiji, so our best bet is to seek out peace right in the middle of our chaos. Guess what? We can have it. Jesus promises peace to all who put him first.

> *You will keep in perfect peace*
> *all who trust in you,*
> *all whose thoughts are fixed on you!*
>
> Isaiah 26:3 NLT

How appealing is it to imagine being unmoved by the stresses in your life? Is it easy or difficult for you to claim this promise for yourself? Ask Jesus to grant you true peace; fix your thoughts on him and watch the rest of the world fade away. When it tries to sneak back in, ask him again.

~ Wednesday May 17, 2017 ~

The sound of being unmoved by the stresses in my life sound very appealing. Almost impossible to fathom. But "I can do all things through Christ who gives me strength." Overall I would say it's been difficult claiming this promise for myself. During pressure from work I can be efficient, calm, professional, and kind and it's all because of Jesus and his strength, not mine. Jesus, I love you and want to get to know you more. I ~~long~~ long to know your heart. Jesus right now I choose to acknowledge you as my Lord and Savior. Please give me true peace. Help me and show me how to fix my eyes, thoughts, and heart on you. I thank you Lord for the gifts of peace, love, and joy. Thank you for the trials, temptations, tests, + circumstances. They have been + are showing me to lean into you further.

LEAVES THAT NEVER WITHER

If you live in a cooler climate, you've probably experienced the gorgeous season that is fall. Each year, the leaves slowly turn to shades of golden yellow, orange, and red. It's a thing of beauty, but eventually, the leaves wither and die, then fall to the ground.

All too often, the same can happen with our relationship with the Lord. We get that initial fire for him; we burn brightly with it, but lose our way and fall away from him. If we keep our trust in him, he tells us that our spiritual leaves will never wither. He wants our lives to be like trees that continually bear fruit.

> It does not fear when heat comes;
> its leaves are always green.
> It has no worries in a year of drought
> and never fails to bear fruit.
>
> Jeremiah 17:8 NIV

Are you bearing good fruit in your spiritual walk, or have you begun to fall away? Plant your roots deeply in him, and let him water your soul.

~ Friday, May 19 2017 ~

I feel like I have been producing a little bit of fruit in my spiritual walk, but I have abandoned it. Like I left it out in the heat for it to get some sun, only it got scorched. Whenever I get hit with pain or something discourages me I feel like I have allowed my fruit's roots to be superficial and they have scattered. Lord help me grow deeper roots in you. I want to be rooted deep down so that rivers of your living water soak into my roots you have given me. Lord my soul needs to be watered more and restored. Refresh me in you Holy Spirit. Come and fill me up with your love, joy + peace to the brim so that I overflow. ♡

WHERE CREDIT IS DUE

You achieve a goal, or you get some wonderful news. The day you've been waiting for has arrived, and you're so excited about it. What is your first reaction? Do you update your status on social media to let your friends know what you've done? Do you call up your mom and tell her the wonderful news?

There's nothing wrong with sharing your excitement with others. But when doing so, be sure to first give the glory and praise to God. He has given you everything you have. Get excited about how good he has been to you. When you're just so happy that you can't help but dance for joy, be sure to give Jesus a twirl too. He wants to celebrate with you!

> *"Give praise to the L*ORD*, proclaim his name;*
> *make known among the nations what he has done,*
> *and proclaim that his name is exalted.*
> *Sing to the L*ORD*, for he has done glorious things;*
> *let this be known to all the world."*
>
> Isaiah 12:4-5 NIV

Are you giving credit where it's due? Be sure to take some time today to thank the Lord for all that he has helped you achieve, and for all that he has given you. He wants to share in your excitement!

Thursday, June 8, 2017   9:08 a.m.
《《≈GOOD MORNING LORD≈》》》

I love you Lord. I love you Holy Spirit.
I love you God. Your trinity is brilliant
and amazing. God thank you for making me.
Even when I have a negative attitude, you
still love and treat me incredibly better
than I deserve. What a Father?! What
a Creator?! What a Savior?! What a Lover?!
I'm in awe of you Lord. You mesmerize
me so stinkin' much《♡》》》 Lord thank you
for giving me a loving and caring family. Thank
you Lord for showing me grace 24/7 and for
forgiving me on the daily. Thank you Lord for healing
me and showing me that You and I ¹and my family + friend want me well.
Thank you Lord for food and for helping me overcome fear
so I can swallow regular again. You are GOOD God! Always!
"My son, pay attention to what I say; listen closely
to my words. Do not let them out of your sight, keep
them WITHIN YOUR HEART; for they are life to those
who find them and health to a man's whole body.
- Proverbs 4:20-22

115

WEARY TO THE CORE

Have you ever been run so ragged that you just didn't know if you could take even one more step? Your calendar is a blur of scheduled activities, your days are full, your every hour is blocked off for this or that, and it's hard to find even a spare minute for yourself. Even your very bones feel weary, and you fall into your bed at night, drained from it all.

There is someone who is ready to catch you when you fall. You might stumble throughout your busy day, but he will never let you hit the floor as you take a tumble. God delights in you! He will direct your every step if you ask him to. He will gladly take you by the hand and guide you.

> *The steps of the God-pursuing ones*
> *follow firmly in the footsteps of the Lord.*
> *And God delights in every step they take to follow him.*
> *If they stumble badly they will still survive,*
> *for the Lord lifts them up with his hands.*

> Psalm 37:23-24 TPT

Are you allowing the Lord to guide your days? Though you may be weary, he has enough energy to get you through it all. Hold out your hand to him today and walk side-by-side with Jesus.

FLIP THE SWITCH

Have you ever walked through your home at night, thinking that you could make it without turning a light on, only to stumble on something unexpectedly set in your path? When you cannot see where you are going, you are likely to get tripped up. On the other hand, your way is obvious when you simply turn on a light.

The Bible tells us that walking in righteousness is just like walking in the bright light of day. But choosing rebellion is like stumbling around in a deep darkness. You never know what hit you until it's already too late.

> *The lovers of God walk on the highway of light,*
> *and their way shines brighter and brighter*
> *until they bring forth the perfect day.*
> *But the wicked walk in thick darkness,*
> *like those who travel in a fog*
> *and yet don't have a clue why they keep stumbling!*
>
> Proverbs 4:18-19 TPT

Are you choosing the light? Is your path brightly lit or are you standing in total darkness? If so, then flip the switch! Pray that you will make wise choices. Seek his wisdom for your life! He wants to shine brightly for you. Let him in, and he will gladly be your eternal light, illuminating your days.

Wednesday June 14, 2017 9:52 a.m.
Yes Lord! Good morning Father! Good morning Holy Spirit! I love you!
Thank you Lord for another day. ♡ Thank you for giving me joy, grace, strength, peace, and energy. Thank you for never leaving me nor forsaking me. Thank you for trials and hard things they are teaching me so much like:
- I can cry out to you and know that you are there comforting me Holy Spirit.
- This is just a test of the many I will face, but
★ I AM GOING THROUGH IT ALL WITH JESUS! ♡★
- I am doing great and with Jesus I overcome.
- I am learning to lean in deeper to Jesus and trust Him. I am walking with Him hand-in-hand through the storms and keeping my gaze fixed on Jesus teaches me to walk on water with Him + burn the boat.
- He knows and I don't. There is beauty in surrender.
- Refining is never easy but always worth it.
- Keep praising + thanking God.   - Get the Word in
- It's okay to ask   119   your heart.
- Keep praying.   for help.   - I'm doing great.

LIGHTHOUSES

There's a good reason why lighthouses were built. For hundreds of years, they've shined brightly across harbors around the world, guiding ships safely to shore. The premise was simple; put the light up high where it can easily be seen.

Jesus is the light of the world. That light wasn't meant to be hidden away. It's meant to be put up high, where everyone can easily see it. And as his followers, we are called to shine brightly for him, in such a way that others can see it for themselves. We don't hide it away; we boldly light the way to Christ.

> "You are the light of the world. A town built on a hill cannot be hidden. Neither do people light a lamp and put it under a bowl. Instead they put it on its stand, and it gives light to everyone in the house."
>
> Matthew 5:14-15 NIV

Don't keep your light for Christ hidden away, bringing it out only when it feels comfortable. Pray that you will have the boldness of faith to be a source of light for everyone with whom you come in contact. Ask the Lord to help you shine brightly so that others may step out of the darkness and join you in the light.

6/19/17
Monday
Love this phrase: "Put the light up high where it can
easily be seen."
- Jesus is not meant to be hidden like a secret -

~~~~~~~~~~~~~~~~~~~~~~~~~~~~

Wednesday June 28, 2017
McLean Household
29 "And now, Lord, behold their ~~threatening~~ threatenings:
and grant unto thy servants, that with
all boldness they may speak thy word,
30 By stretching forth thine hand to heal; and
that signs and wonders may be done by the
name of the holy child Jesus."
Acts 4:29-30

NEW LIFE

Have you ever laid in bed at night, thinking over past wrongdoings and beating yourself up over decisions you made years ago? If so, you are not alone. Women can be incredibly hard on themselves, asking for near perfection.

There is good news for us all! Once we accept Christ as our Savior, we are made new. There is no need to continue to berate ourselves for the choices of the past. He has washed away our sins and made us clean. We don't have to look at life from our former point of view because our old lives are gone and new ones have begun!

> The LORD is good to all,
> and his mercy is over all that he has made.
>
> Psalm 145:9 ESV

Release your past to the Lord. If you struggle to get past a mistake you once made, ask him for help in forgiving yourself. You have been made new in the eyes of the Lord! There is so much freedom in this knowledge! Enjoy it!

MY THOUGHTS

LOSING TO GAIN

The key to growing in your faith is simple. There must be less of *us* in order to have more of God. To allow more of his presence into our lives, we must give up more of ourselves. We need to place our lives before him as an offering and give him our all.

The world would say that giving up ourselves is a loss. We've been taught for years that we must put ourselves first. Our fellow man would say that we need to make ourselves a priority. But oh, are they missing out! When we give ourselves over completely to God, we get to share in his glory and in his great joy. Setting aside our earthly pleasures for heavenly treasures means we gain a lot more than what this world could ever offer us.

> *"If you try to hang on to your life, you will lose it. But if you give up your life for my sake, you will save it."*
>
> Matthew 16:25 NLT

What desires do you find yourself holding onto? Empty yourself of the desires of your flesh and allow God to fill you with his presence. You won't feel a lack. In fact, it will overflow in your life, spilling out everywhere for others to see!

MY THOUGHTS

....

....

....

....

....

....

....

....

....

....

....

....

....

....

....

IN SUNSHINE AND STORM

It's easy to feel happy on a sunny day, when all is well, the birds are singing, and life is going along swimmingly. But what happens when waters are rougher, bad news comes, or the days feel just plain hard?

God wants us to feel gladness when times are good. He has made each and every day. We are called to rejoice in all of them whether good or bad. Happiness is determined by our circumstances, but true joy comes when we can find the silver linings, hidden in our darkest hours—when we can sing his praises no matter what. We don't know what the future holds for us here on earth, but we can find our delight in the knowledge that our eternity is set in beauty.

> When times are good, be happy;
> but when times are bad, consider this:
> God has made the one as well as the other.
> Therefore, no one can discover
> anything about their future.
>
> Ecclesiastes 7:14 NIV

Is your happiness determined by your circumstance? Pray that you will discover true joy in our Creator. Ask him to give you a deep and abiding satisfaction in each day that goes beyond human understanding.

MY THOUGHTS

POWER
WITHOUT LIMIT

There is only so much that we can accomplish in our own strength. We plow through our tasks, and we can get a lot done. But we are limited in our power.

God has no limit in what he can do! If we ask him to work in our lives, there's no stopping the amazing things that will happen! We can accomplish more than we'd ever think to ask for. The best part is that he *wants* to do it for us. It's not a chore for him or another task to cross off his list so that you'll stop pestering him.

> *To him who is able to do immeasurably more than all we ask or imagine, according to his power that is at work within us, to him be glory in the church and in Christ Jesus throughout all generations, for ever and ever! Amen.*
>
> Ephesians 3:20-21 NIV

Ask the Lord for bigger and bolder things. Pray that he will give you the supernatural ability you need to accomplish all that's before you. His power is without limits, and he will extend it to you if you'll only ask him for it!

MY THOUGHTS

WE HAVE TIME

Time is one of those things we never seem to have enough of. Many of our days can feel like a race against the clock to get everything done. We seem to lack the time we need for even the most important things—things like being in God's Word, spending intentional time with loved ones, or volunteering to help those in need.

At the end of the day, there is one reality we must remember: we have time for what we make time for. It's easy to feel busy, but what are we truly busying ourselves with? Are we finding time to spend browsing social media or watching re-runs of our favorite TV shows? Are we finding time to take a long shower or sleep for a few extra minutes in the morning? None of those things are necessarily *wrong*, but if we feel pressed for time and are unable to spend time with the Lord, we may need to rethink where our time goes.

> *Be careful how you live. Don't live like fools, but like those who are wise. Make the most of every opportunity in these evil days. Don't act thoughtlessly, but understand what the Lord wants you to do.*
>
> Ephesians 5:15-17 NLT

Take a good hard look at your day today. How can you spend your time wisely—in a way that will make the most of the moments and opportunities you have.

~ Monday evening December 18, 2017 ~
I love you Lord! Praise and honor to
You! All of my heart is yours! ♡

→ -We have time for what we make time for. —

At the start of the day I want the
real You Jesus. During the day I want
to stay close in communication and
have Your presence all around me and go
before me. At the end of the day I
want to reflect back on what all Jesus taught me,
how well did I love people with God's love,
how many laughs I had and who I shared them
with, prayers I shared and need to keep speaking
life into, seeing what promises came to pass, tears shed,

NO CONDEMNATION

Most of us know the story of the woman caught in adultery. One of the intriguing moments was when Jesus was questioned about whether or not the woman should be stoned. His response is to stoop down and start writing in the dirt. Jesus' action of stooping in the dirt defines one interpretation of the word *grace*.

As they all stood casting judgement, Jesus removed himself from the accusers, stooping low and occupying himself elsewhere. It spoke volumes about his lack of participation in the crowd's judgement. Because of Jesus' distraction, the eyes of the onlookers were drawn off the woman, perhaps lifting a portion of her shame. With their attention focused on Jesus, he said the words that saved the woman's life: "Let him who has never sinned cast the first stone." One by one, the accusers walked away.

> Straightening up, Jesus said to her, "Woman, where are they? Did no one condemn you?" She said, "No one, Lord." And Jesus said, "I do not condemn you either. Go. From now on sin no more."

John 8:10-11 NASB

Jesus was the only one qualified to stone the adulterous woman. This is a beautiful foreshadowing of the redemption he later brought to all sinners. Beloved, Jesus is the only one qualified to condemn you, and he chose to condemn himself instead. You are free and clean because of the grace of Jesus Christ. Thank him for it today.

MY THOUGHTS

PERSEVERANCE

Do you remember when you first decided to follow Christ? Maybe you felt like a huge weight was being lifted off you, or that the peace and joy you'd been searching for was finally yours. You were filled with excitement in your newfound life, and you felt ready to take on the world in the name of Jesus.

Following God may come easy at first. We accept him into our lives and are swept into his love with incredible hope. But as time goes on, old temptations return, and threaten to shake our resolve. The confidence we felt in our relationship at first lessens as we wonder if we have what it takes to stick it out in this Christian life.

> Do not throw away this confident trust in the Lord. Remember the great reward it brings you! Patient endurance is what you need now, so that you will continue to do God's will. Then you will receive all that he has promised.
>
> Hebrews 10:35-36 NLT

Have you lost the confidence you had at first? Step boldly forward into all that God has for you. He will accomplish what he has promised. When following him gets hard, press in even harder and remember that you will be richly rewarded for your perseverance.

· Sunday, May 6, 2018 ·

Yes Lord. The more I press into You, the more I get attacked by the enemy, but I don't care. I love You God! I love You Holy Spirit! I love Your will Lord over my own. I want You! I choose You! Lord please help me with keeping my eyes on You. Lord I ask for patient endurance so that I will continue to do God's will. Lord I choose to press into Yous even harder! Only your opinion matters. I will trust You Lord! I believe that You will accomplish everything you have promised me! You're GOOD ALL THE TIME!

"The Lord will fight for you; you need only to be still." -Exod. 14:14

"Do not throw away this confident trust in the Lord. Remember the great reward it brings you! Patient endurance is what you need now, so that you will continue to do God's will. Then you will receive all that he has promised." -Hebrews 10:35-36 NLT

I will praise You my God, my Father! I will give You my God, my Father. With every breath I am given, I will give back to You in praise. ♡ Yes Lord. ♡♡♡♡♡♡

135

PERFECT LOVE

Does anyone know the *real* you? The you that hasn't been edited or exaggerated?

Putting up a false front in our relationships is a direct expression of our own fear. When we are afraid to be truly known, we lose out on the most incredible gift that can be given in relationship—honest love. We sacrifice genuine relationship on the altar of our own insecurity and fear.

> We know the love that God has for us, and we trust that love. God is love. Those who live in love live in God, and God lives in them. This is how love is made perfect in us: that we can be without fear on the day God judges us, because in this world we are like him.
>
> 1 John 4:16-17 NCV

Are you afraid to be fully known? Lay down your need to be perceived as perfect, and allow yourself to be loved for who you truly are. Let your fear be washed away by the perfect love of a perfect God.

MY THOUGHTS

THIRST FOR PURE WATER

Have you ever noticed that the more consistently you drink water, the more your body thirsts for it? And the less you drink water, the less you consciously desire it. Though you still need water to live, you become satisfied with small amounts of it disguised in other foods and drinks. But for a body that has become accustomed to pure water on a daily basis, only straight water will quench its thirst.

The same principle applies to God's presence in our lives. The more we enter his presence, the more we long to stay there. The more we sit at his feet and listen to what he has to say, the more we need his Word to continue living. But if we allow ourselves to become satisfied with candy-coated truth and second hand revelation, we will slowly begin to lose our hunger for the pure, untainted presence of the living God.

> *I want more than anything*
> *to be in the courtyards of the Lord's Temple.*
> *My whole being wants*
> *to be with the living God.*
>
> Psalm 84:2 NCV

Does your entire being long to be with God? Press into Jesus until you can no longer be satisfied with anything less than the purest form of his presence. Cultivate your hunger and your fascination with him until you crave him. Spend your life feasting on his truth, knowing his character, and adoring his heart.

MY THOUGHTS

Colour Conference   10/27/16

Priscilla Shirer → The Secret of Beholding

• Luke 24:13-15

* God wants to meet with us right in our
Circumstance(s).
                    → added before something
                                    big happens
  — The secret of Beholding and leaning in
  and being aware that something great is
  about to happen.

Secret 1) The greatest miracle God can do is
  to open our eyes and change our heart
  in the circumstances. Glimpses of His
  glory and favor → the abundant life.
  Lean in and be expectant.
  Isaiah 43:18-19
  ↳ Behold, I am going to do something new!
  — Allow your spiritual radar to pick up
     God's activity and lean in and get
  in tune with what He wants to do in our
  life.

When we are in over our head, like water
of life, we are stilled, equipped and fitted
with what is necessary to see because
of the Holy Spirit.
Exod. 14→ Do not be afraid and see's
Keep your eyes open for the salvation
of the Lord. (Moses and the people
of Israel)

Luke
act 24:13 2) The Secret to going home.
↳ Jesus encountered 2 men after they left
Passover and went home.
- The secret of expecting God to
invade our lives.
* Jesus only had a little over a month
left on earth to ~~act~~ live and He chose
to take time to connect and collaborate
with people individually.
- Don't break your covenant with the Lord.

Gen. 15 Yahweh put Abraham to sleep
so that He could come to earth
in a human form to walk among
the covenant of the broken
animal pieces. (God did want
Man's help for His plans) ✓ All glory
to God!

- There's a problem if we are doing
more talking then listening.

* When we talk nothing happens. When He
talks worlds happen. *

* When you invite Jesus to sit on the
throne of your life and make decision
that will create your life to please Him.

~ Intimacy and communication flourish here ~

* The Holy Spirit is the steady anchor
that keeps you ~~steady~~ steady, confident, and courageous
when nothing else is steady.

MY THOUGHTS

MY THOUGHTS